The Birds' Journey to Mount Qaf

Hooda Shawa Qaddumi

The Birds' Journey to Mount Qaf

Inspired by Farid uddin al-Attar's
Mantiq at-Tayr (*Conference of the Birds*)

Original illustrations by
Vanessa Hodgkinson

SAQI
London San Francisco

To Nabil

ISBN 10: 0-86356-443-7
ISBN 13: 978-0-86356-443-7

First published in 2006 by Saqi Books

A full CIP record for this book is available from the British Library.
A full CIP record for this book is available from the Library of Congress.

Printed in Lebanon by Chemaly & Chemaly
Binding: Fouad El-Baayno Bookbinders

SAQI

26 Westbourne Grove, London W2 5RH
825 Page Street, Suite 203, Berkeley, California 94710
www.saqibooks.com

The Birds' Journey to Mount Qaf

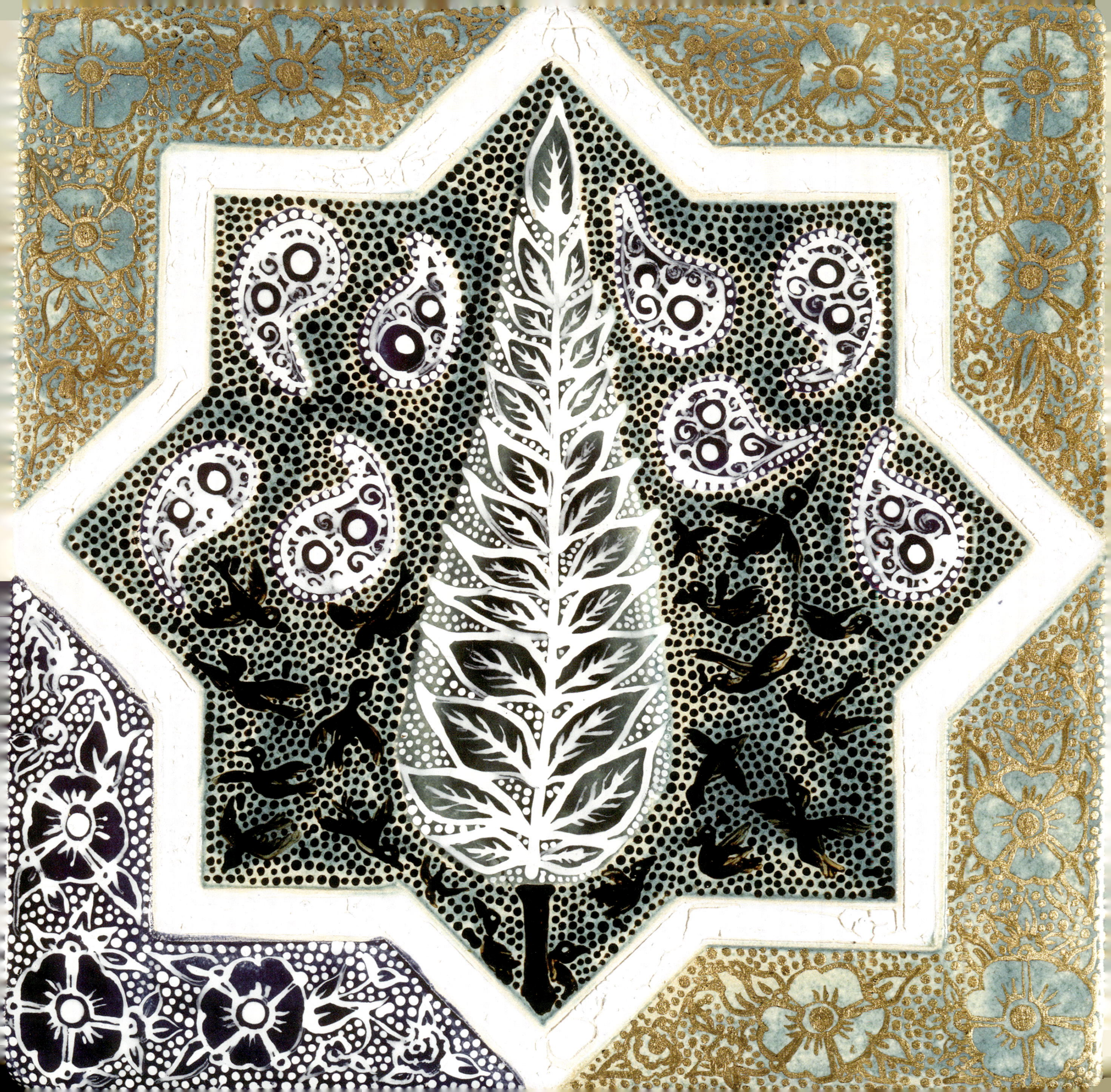

All the birds of the world gathered in a bustan one day,
And declared: We live in times of woe and dismay,
Where chaos, tyranny and oppression reign,
All nations have a ruler, king or sovereign.
Therefore, a great wise leader we must seek,
Who is righteous and strong, yet merciful and meek.
A benevolent ruler, who treats us with care,
To lead us, to guide us through times rough and fair.

While the birds deliberated how to set out on their quest,
The hoopoe fluttered forward with his crowned crest:

Greetings from King Solomon's guide and confidant herein
Whom God chose to reign over bird, beast and jinn
And empowered with command over wind in valleys and mountain peaks,
And the language of birds enabled him to speak.

I, who Solomon sought among the rest,
To deliver his messages, he chose the best.
To Balqis, Queen of Sheba, I was dispatched,
To carry an entrusted message unmatched.

And after she read out my secret letter,

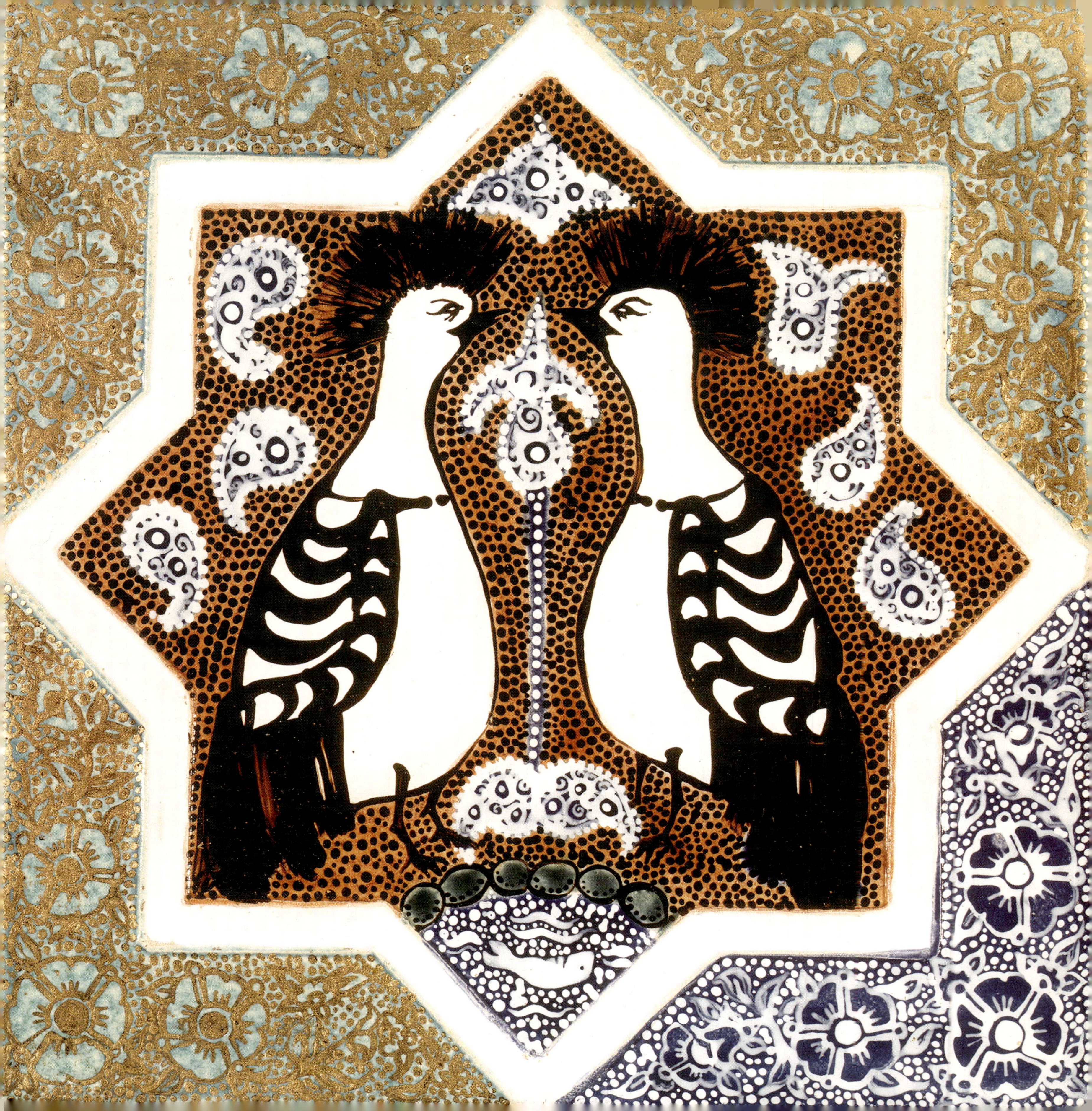

She abandoned the worship of the sun forever!

Many days, weeks and years flying I have spent,
To India, Sind and China I was sent,

Past oceans deep, lakes and desert sands,
Over mountains, valleys and arid lands,

Carrying stories, messages and secret letters,
Delivering news on important matters.

It was one night while soaring in the Chinese sky,
I heard people talk of a great bird that flew by,

Called Simurgh, the greatest bird alive,
Who dwells on Mount Qaf, where he is said to thrive,
Upon a giant mountain unlike any other seen, covered with trees,
Beyond Samarkand, across seven valleys and seven seas.

It is rumoured that on one moonlit night,

As the great Simurgh flew over the city, a wondrous sight,
One golden feather from his tail floated down
And carried by the winds, softly fell to the ground,

Right and left
North and south
East and west

And whoever saw that shining feather
Was enchanted by its magical colour.

Men, women and children fell under its spell,
And rumour spread like fire impossible to quell.
All were struck by awe and strong desire
To meet the great Simurgh, with his untold power.

The hoopoe continued to speak self-importantly:
Let us leave, dear friends, depart this land instantly

And seek the Simurgh in faraway Samarkand,
To choose him as the leader of our faithful band,
For a King of Birds surely reigns supreme,
On distant Mount Qaf, a truth not a dream.

The birds looked at each other in despair:

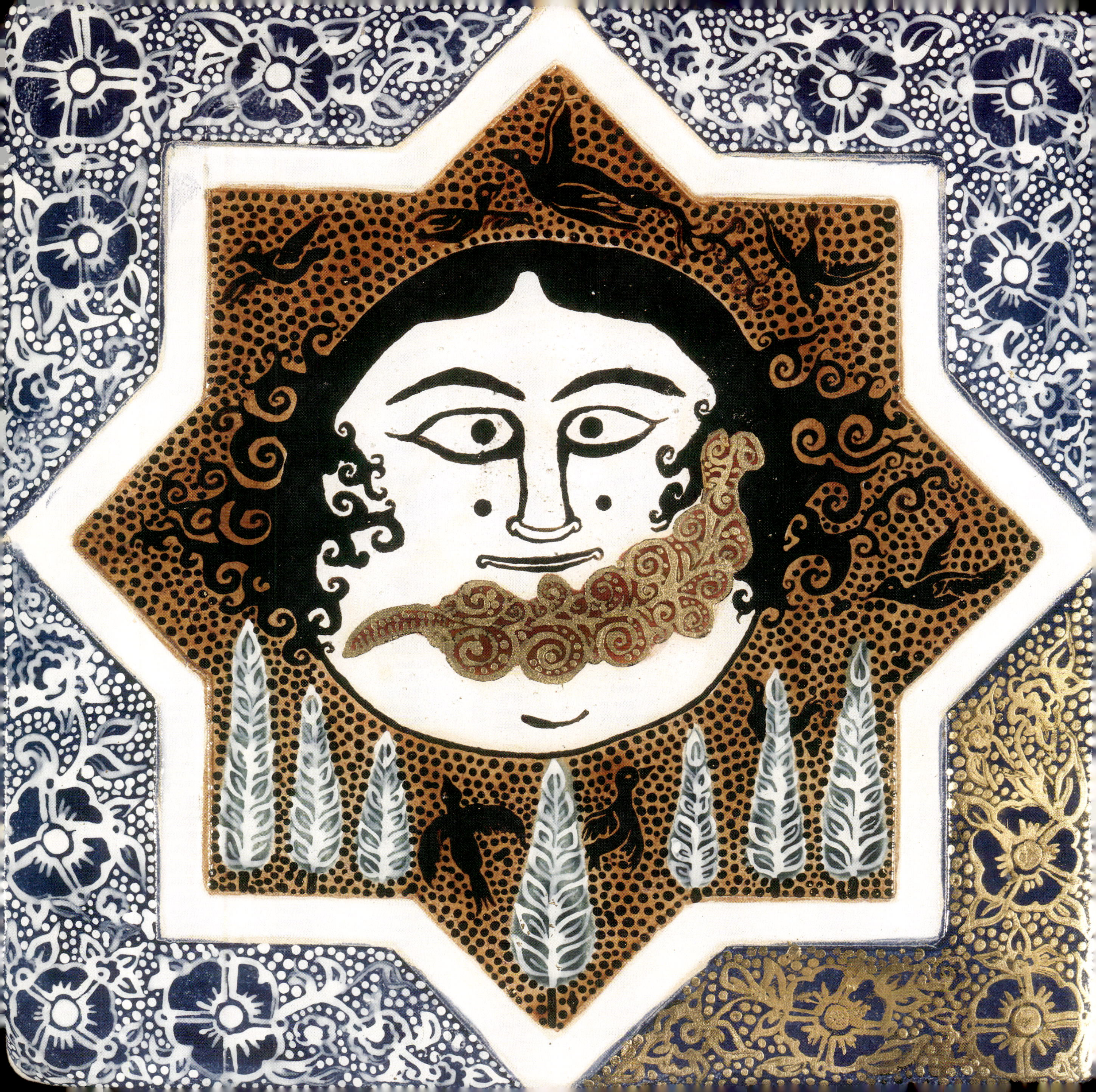

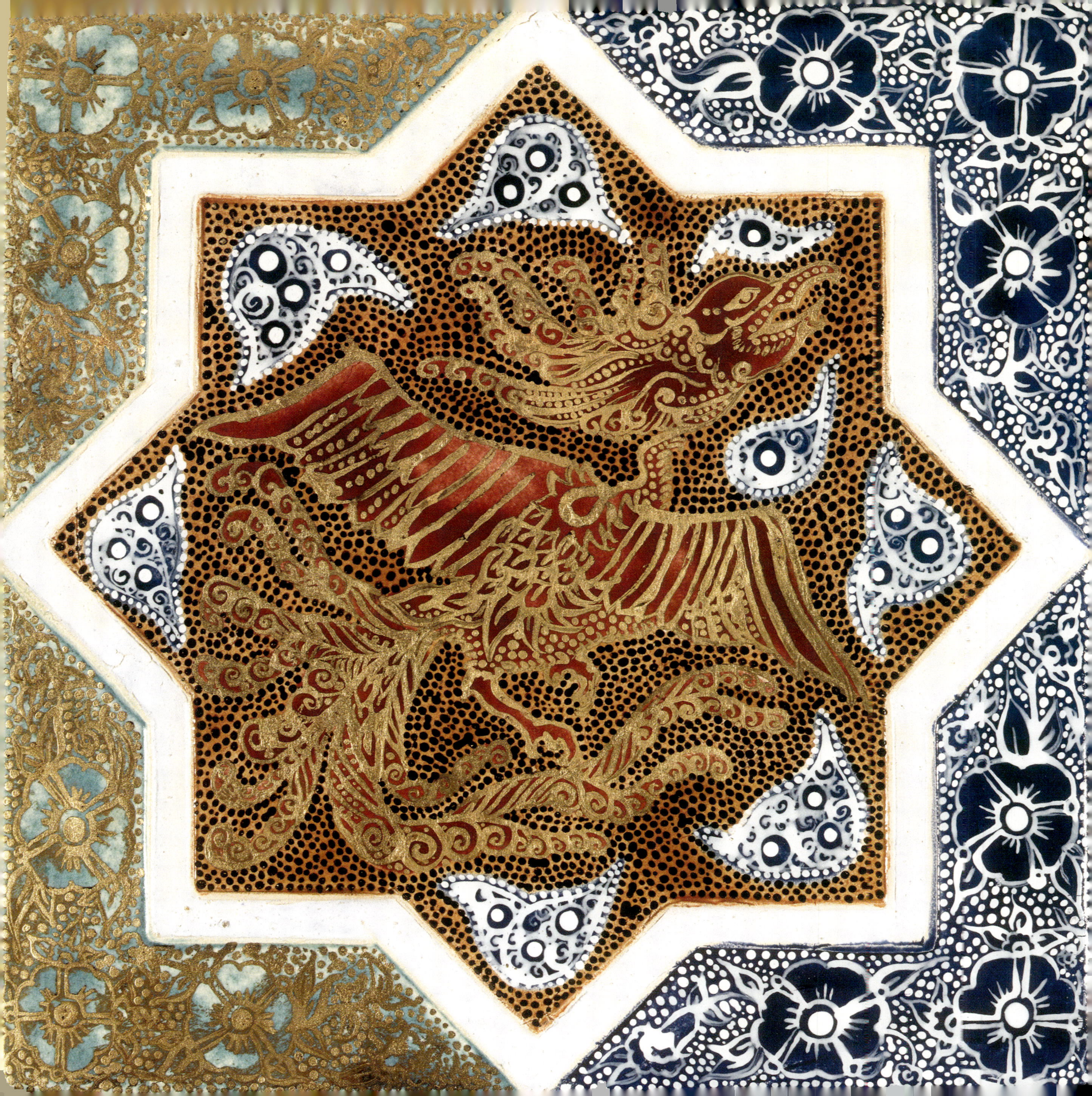

Who is willing to abandon his accustomed lair
And leave his comfortable abode
To go to distant lands, some hot and some cold?

For here, we are happy and content,
And with our lot cannot lament.

So stepping forward with excuses,
One by one, each bird politely refuses.

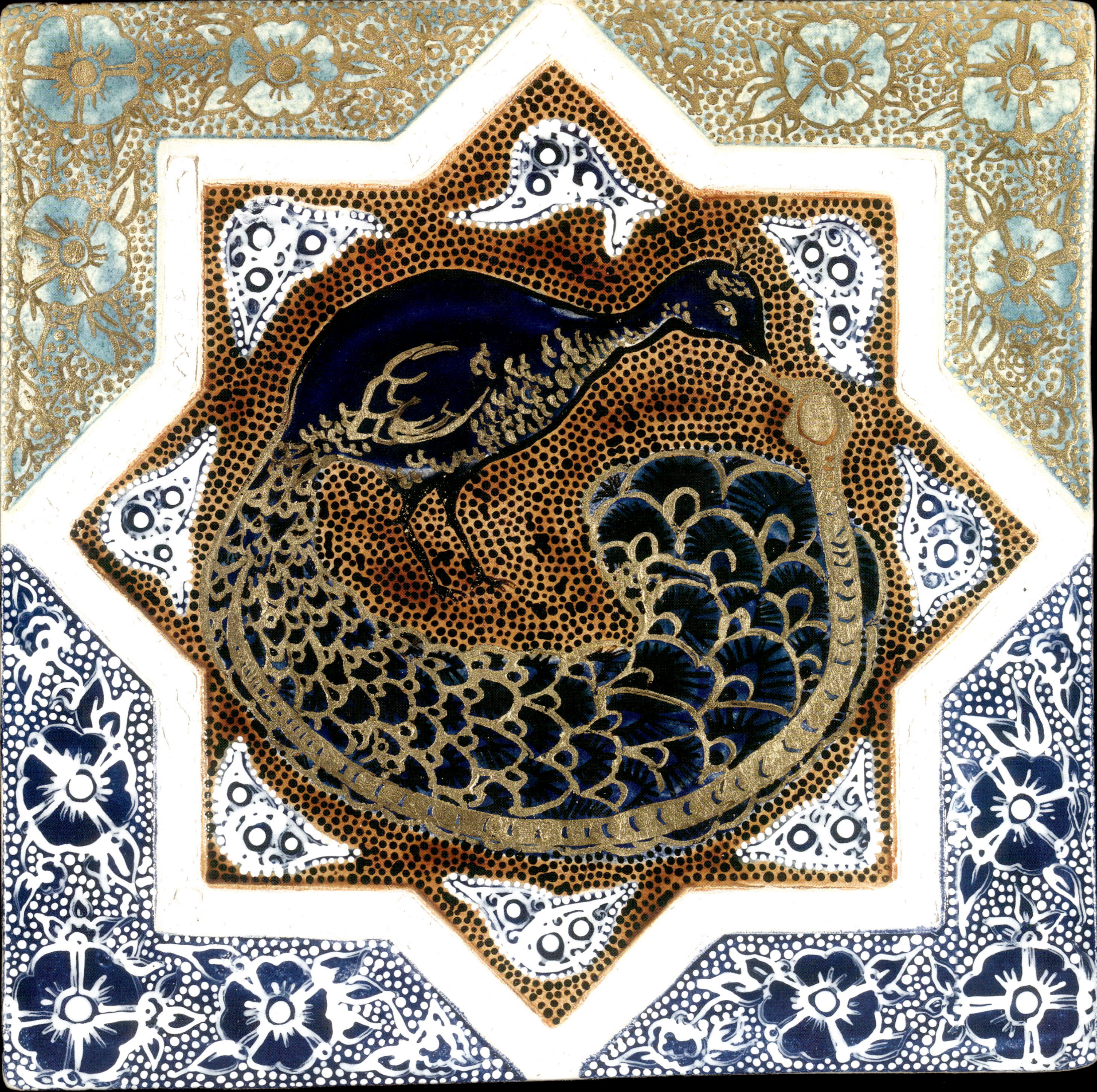

The Peacock's Excuse

The Peacock came forward bursting with pride,
Strutting in lapis lazuli from side to side.
His gorgeous tail displayed a thousand eyes,
He said, as he looked around in feigned surprise:

Has anyone seen a more beautiful sight?
Does not my beauty surpass visionary delight?
Am *I* not the fairest of all birds around?
Aren't *I* worthy to be your king enthroned?

The Hoopoe's Answer

Peacock, your arrogance and great vanity
Shall surely be the cause of your insanity.
Rule of birds cannot be with pomp and pride.
Let values, not vanity be your guide.

Abandon your beloved mirror for a while,
Look deeper around you, not at your reflected smile,
And I am confident, you shall see,
A much more beautiful world than thee!

The Nightingale's Excuse

The love-smitten nightingale sings the sweetest notes:
The orchard echoes with melodies pouring from my throat.

And lovers' hearts resonate to my honey-sweet songs,
But to the red rose my heart only belongs.

She smiles for me alone,
She laughs for me only,
With her beautiful colour I am enchanted,
No other in my heart can be implanted.

The Hoopoe's Answer

The red rose is truly a glorious sight,
Her crimson perfumed petals are pure delight.

Yet each rose is destined to wither and wane,
Her fleeting beauty does not remain.
And have you not felt her needle-sharp thorns?
Beware her laughter, for deep down she scorns.

Forsake the morning rose, her beauty is entwined
With sorrow, tears and heartbreak combined.

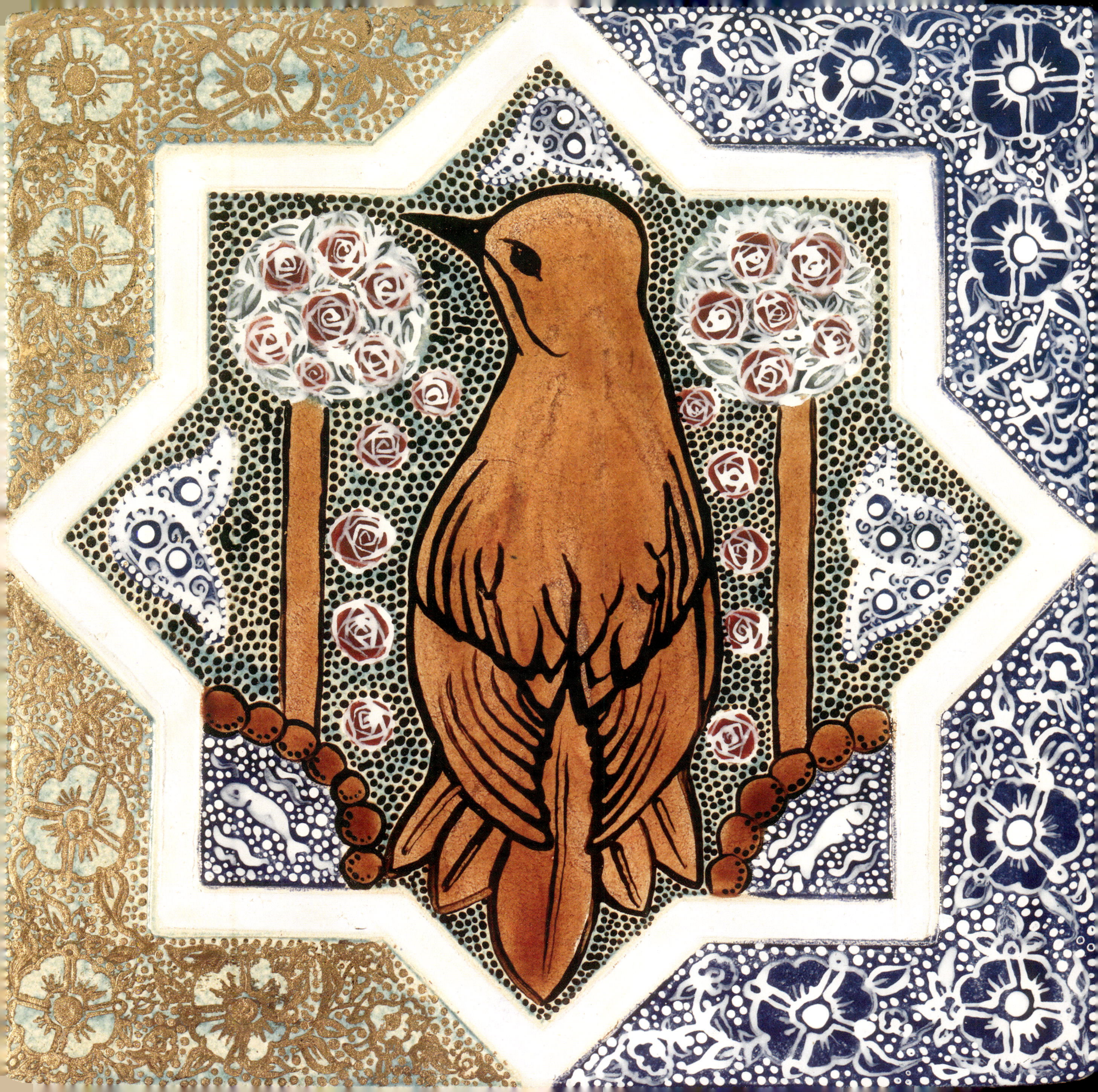

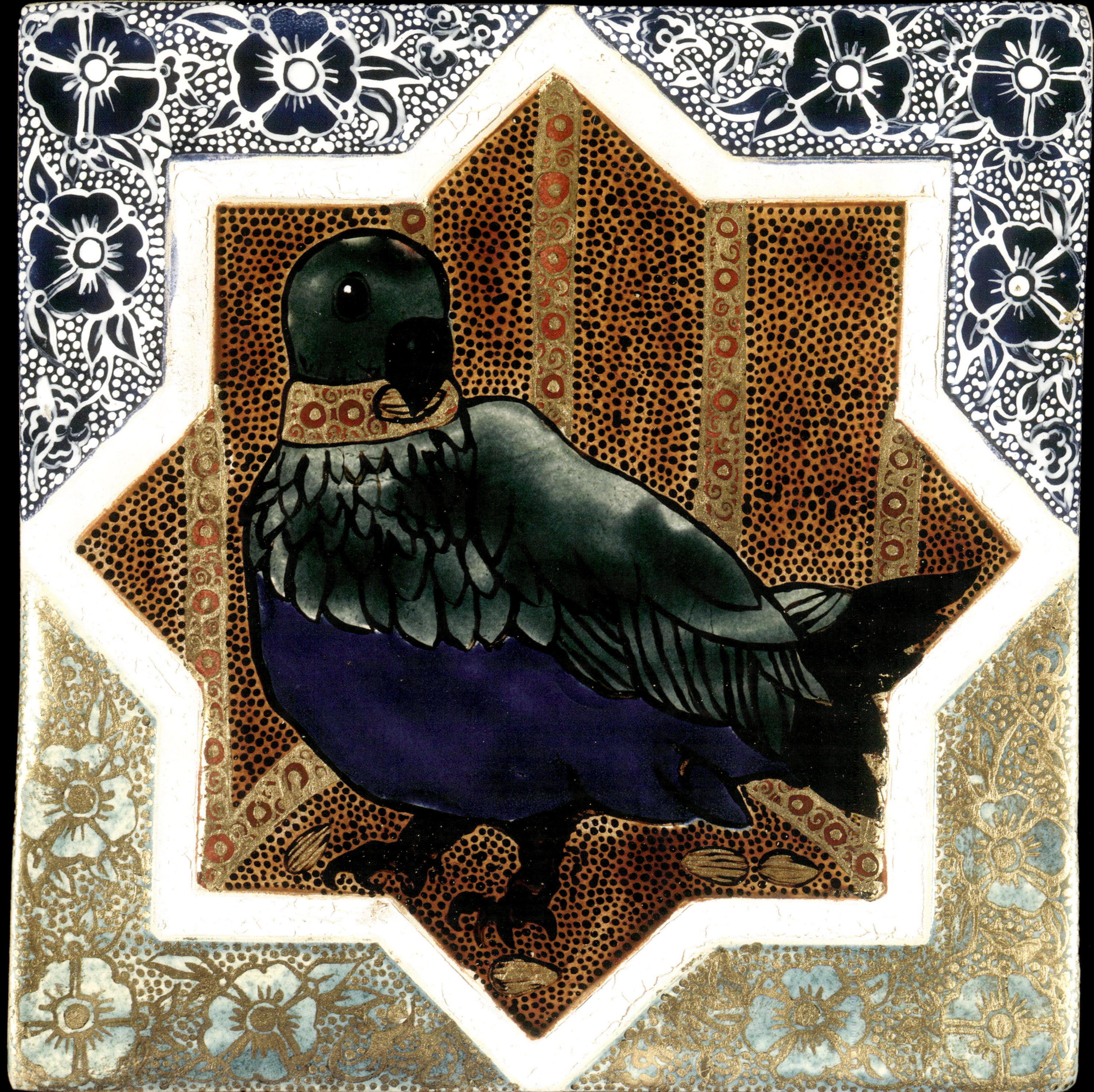

The Parrot's Excuse

The pretty parrot was the next bird to speak,
Sugared almonds spilling from her beak,

Around her neck a band of burnished gold,
She shrieked: a gilded cage is my abode.

Why leave this sweet life
To one of hardship and strife?

The Hoopoe's Answer

You silly, spoilt, selfish bird,
To accept such chains, you must be absurd.

These golden chains around your neck
Your dreams suffocate, your ambitions wreck.

And he who soars in open plains
Cannot tolerate even golden reins.

Don't be a foolish bird. Be wise,
Your precious freedom never compromise.

The Duck's Excuse

The Duck waddled forth so heavily;
My abode is rivers, streams or sea.

How can I leave the crystal shore
On a trip where terrible thirst I must endure?

Would a wise man abandon a guaranteed prey
To chase a mere mirage on a desert way?

The Hoopoe's Answer

Sometimes cruel hardships have to be endured,
For patience and tolerance must be secured.
And beware friendly water that within its folds
Lurk dangers and hidden horrors untold.

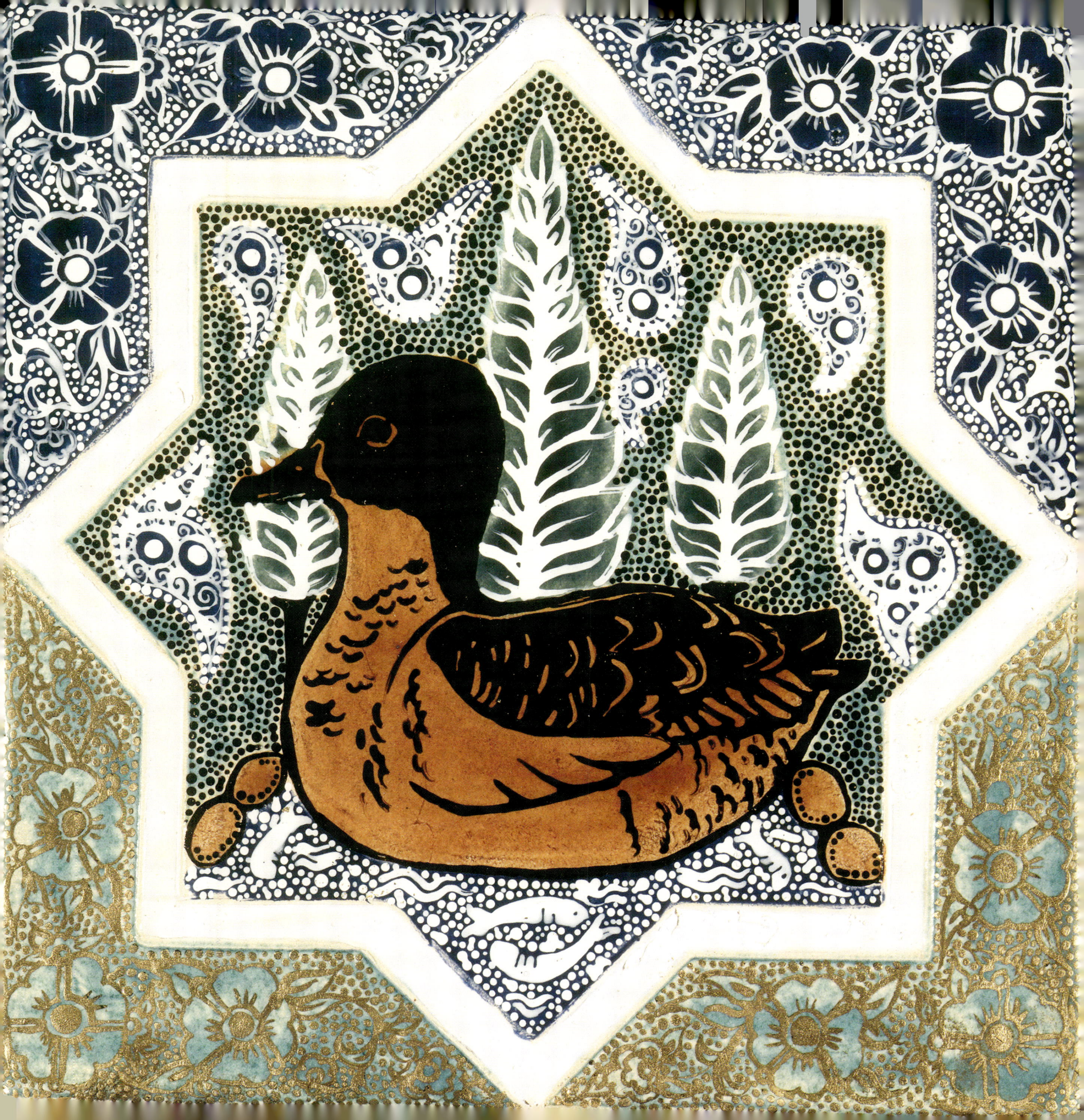

The Partridge's Excuse

The partridge approached and meekly said:
My passion is for shiny pearls and rubies red,

Gold, glitter, and precious gems,
Sparkling emeralds and diadems.

No one can quench my deep desire,
For jewelled stones that glow like fire.

The Hoopoe's Answer

Your shameful life of hoarding gold
Has hardened your heart, rendered it cold.

What are jewels deprived of hues but dull stones?
For such sinful acts of greed, you should atone.

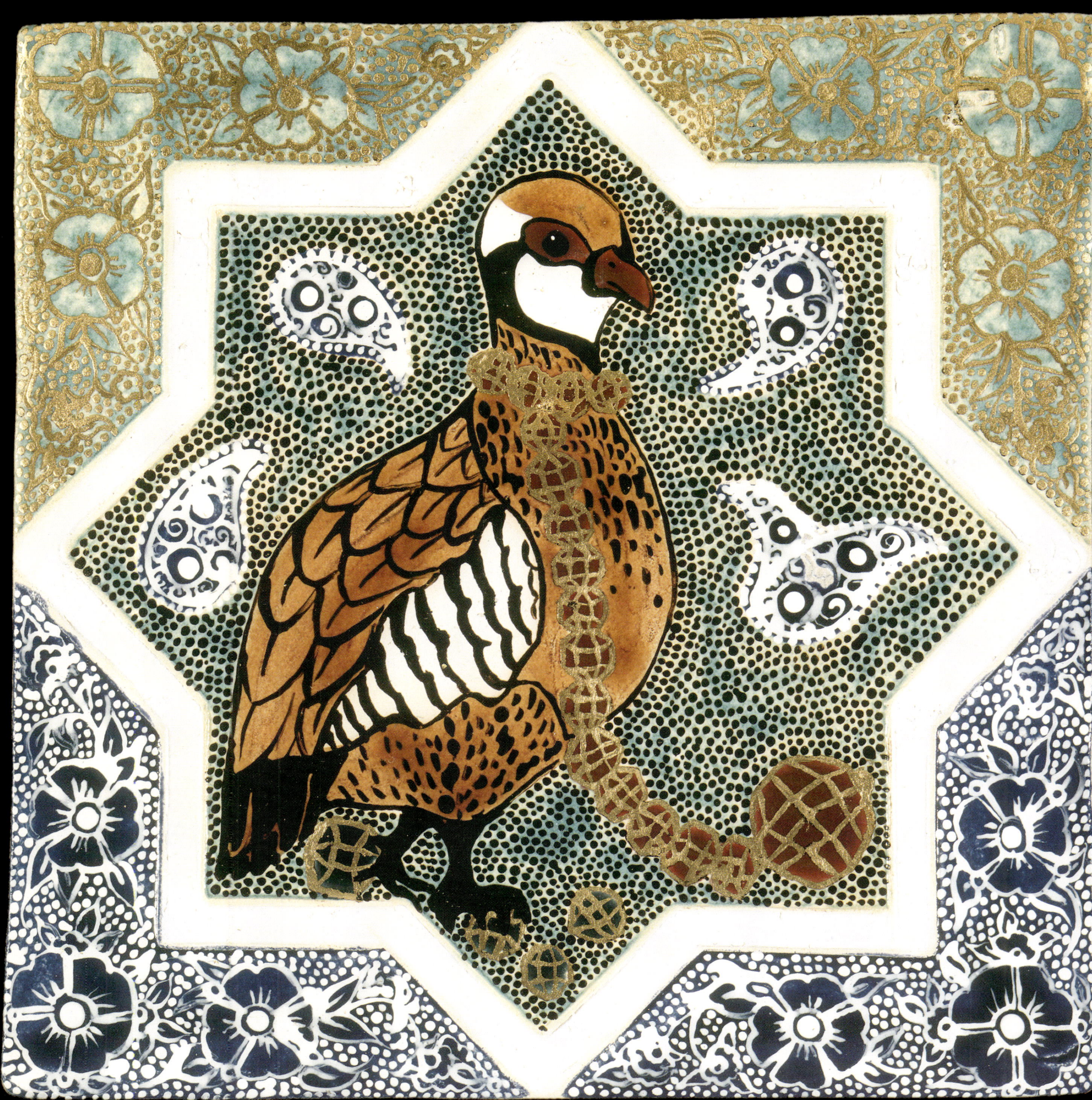

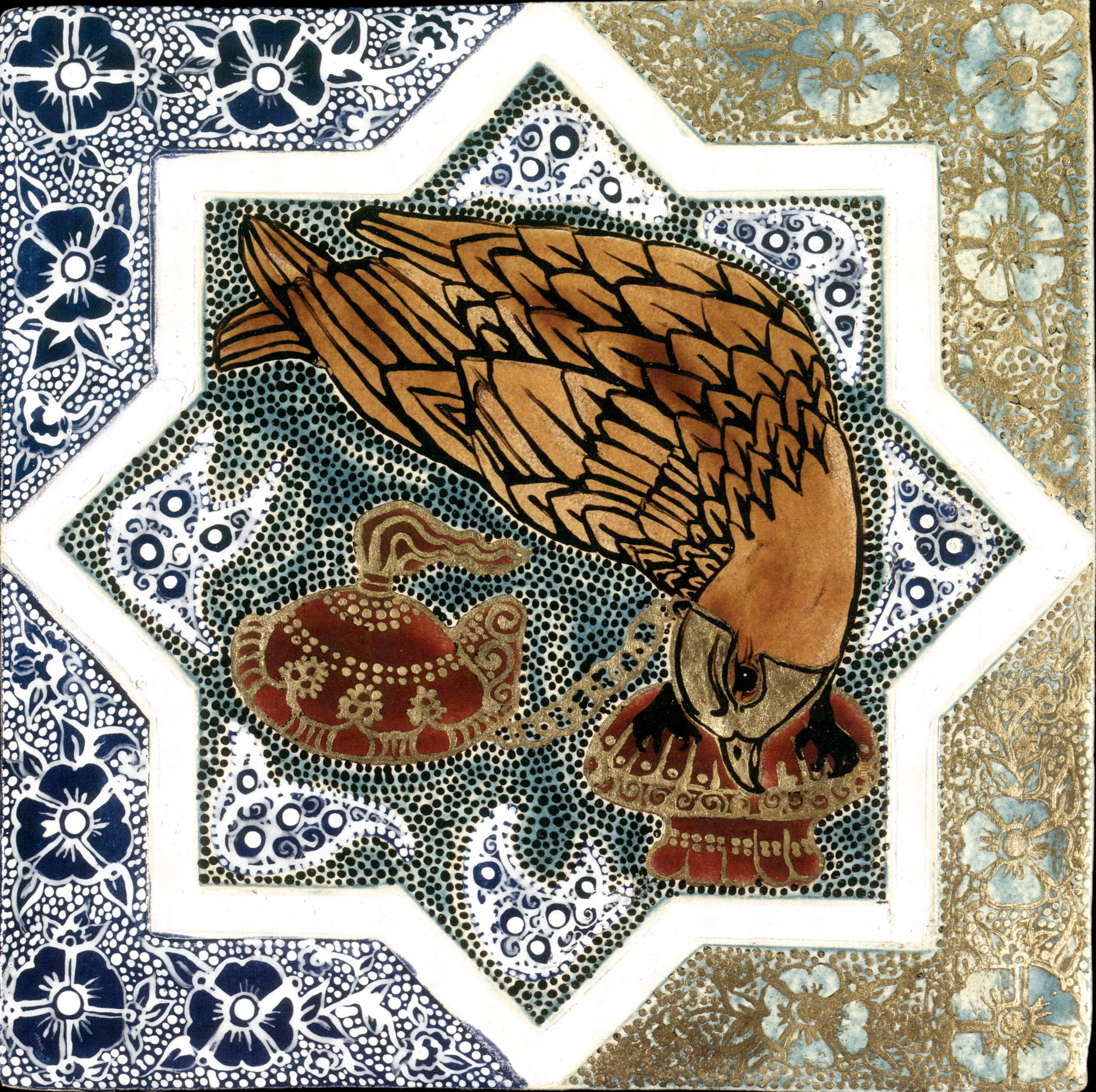

The Hawk's Excuse

The Hawk then mightily descended,
Wings abreast and chest extended:
My company is the fist of the Sultan, or by his side
My entourage is that of kings and princes as they ride.

I accompany the sultan on his foray,
On his hunting trips I lead the way.

It fills me with pride, joy and delight
To join him morning, noon and night.

The Hoopoe's Answer

Hawk, captive of royalty, prisoner of palace,
Has it never crossed your mind, even once,
That the Sultan may swiftly replace you, given a chance,
With a younger, faster, substitute,
After which you shall be left destitute?
How many ambitious men I have seen
Who owned the lands and ruled the realm,

Humbly stumble from great heights
And plummet down after such might.

Abandon this pompous life of worldly kings,
Beware the perils their power brings,

And watch out for those who display amicability
That can quickly transfer to dangerous hostility.

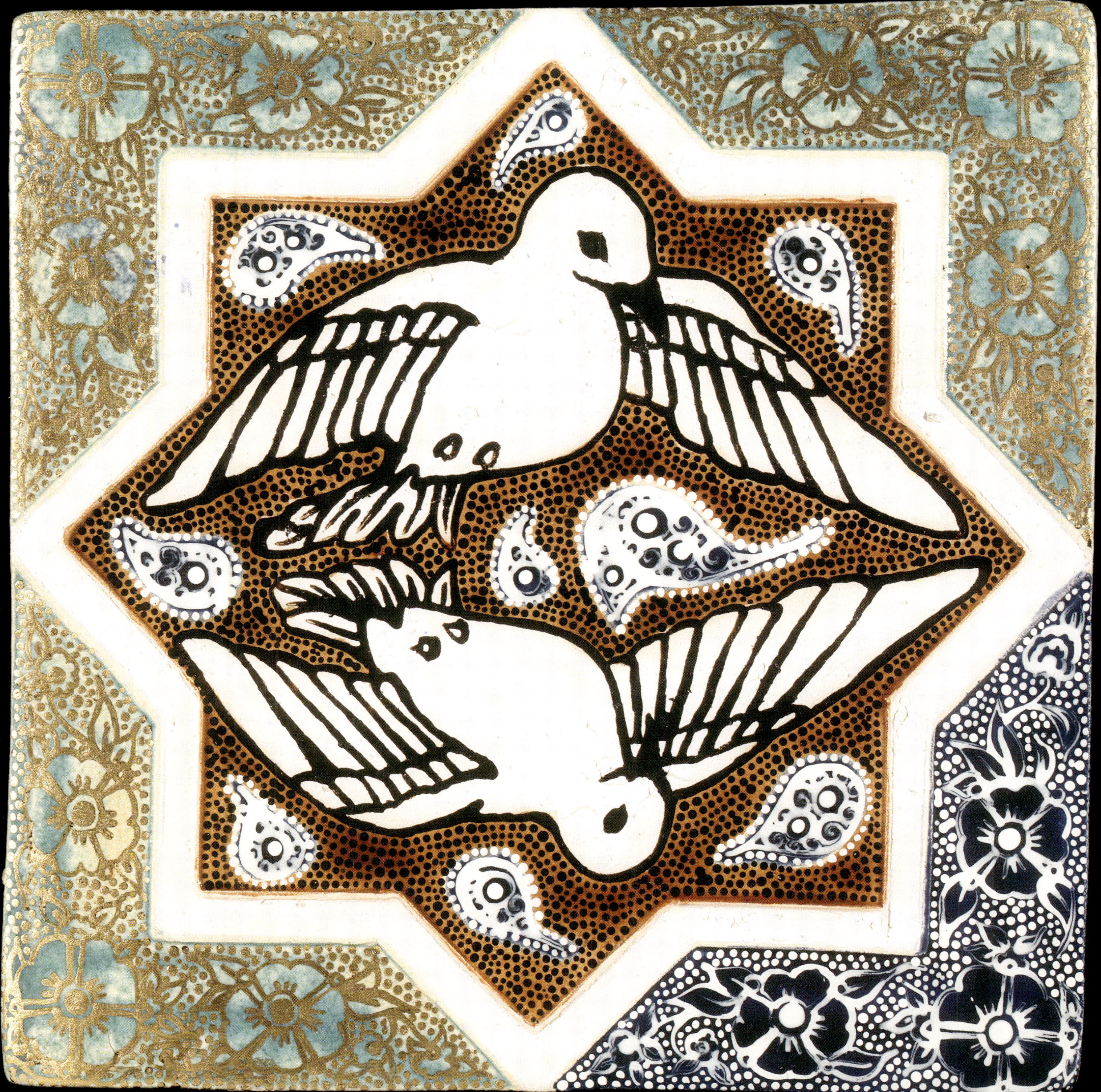

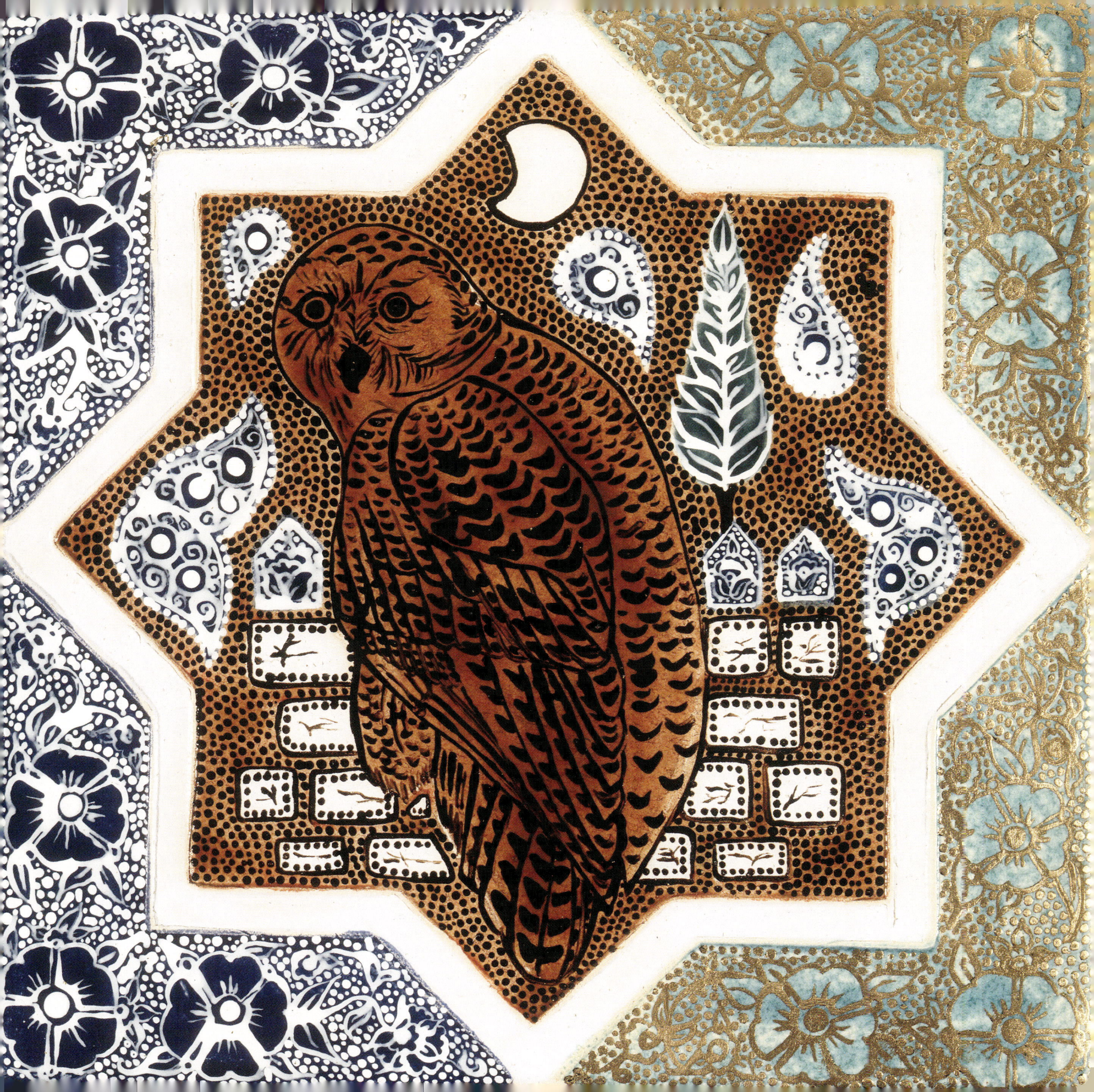

The Owl's Excuse

The Owl then shrieked in crazy voices,
Her hoots filled the air with shrilling noises:

I venture out when there's no light,
I adore my solitude in the depth of night,

My home is ruins, wrecks and desolate places.
How shall I soar in the sky in open spaces
In daylight accompanied with a group of strangers?
I'd rather die than face such dangers.

The Hoopoe's Answer

Owl, lover of darkness and solitary gloom,
Abandon your existence of eternal doom.

Seek the open plains and soar on high
Beyond the frontiers of the azure sky.

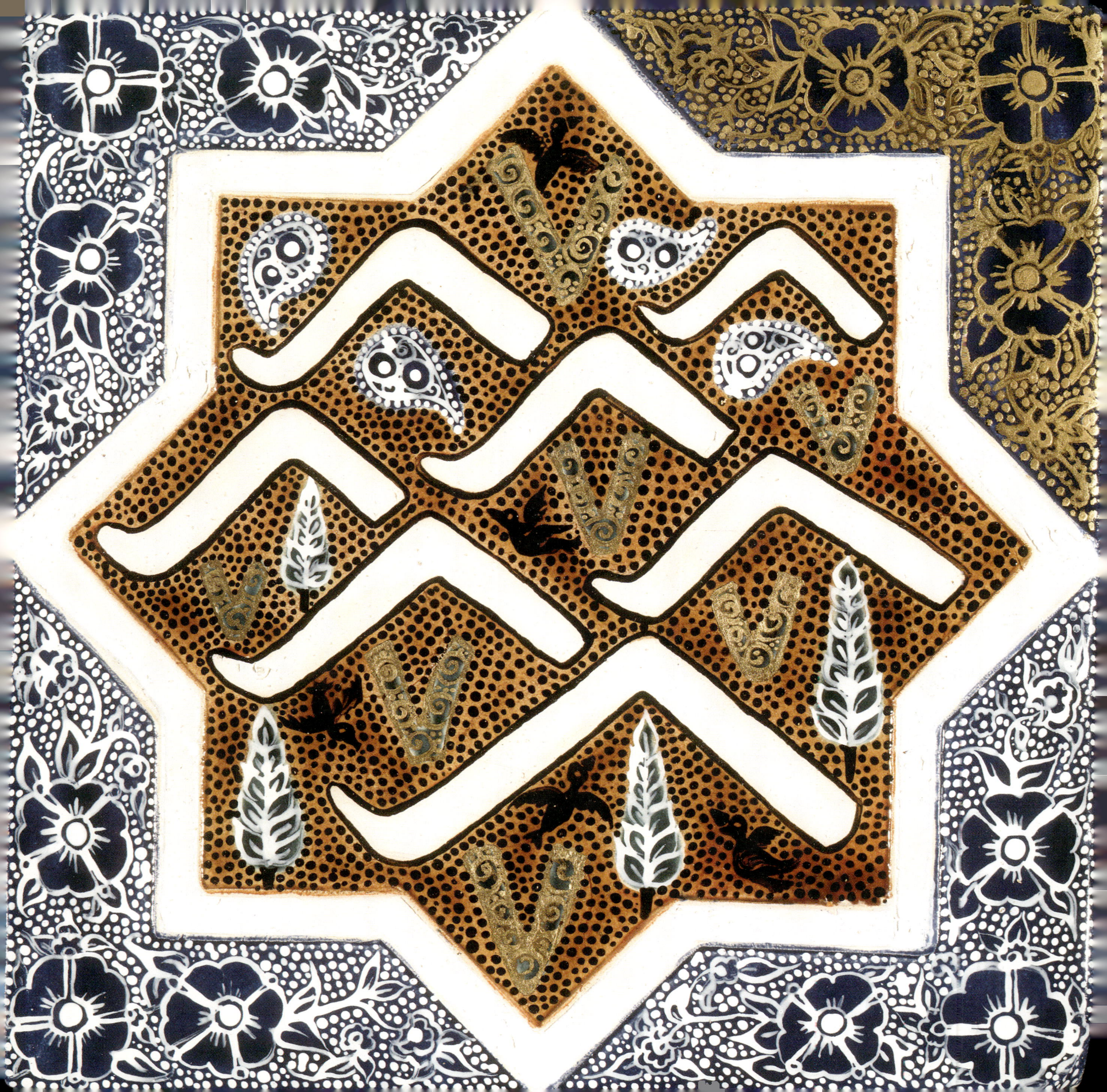

The Quest

After the group heard the hoopoe's debate,
They were convinced by the arguments he had made.

They determined to leave behind everything,
To soar the skies to meet the Simurgh king.

The hoopoe then proceeded to say:
Beware my friends, the journey to Qaf is a difficult way.

Many dangers and perils we shall confront on the path,
Arousing many demons and monsters wrath.

Flying through strong storms and windy days,
Soaring through both freezing nights and burning rays

And across seven dangerous valleys we must fly.
Only the brave patient pilgrim can survive.

Yet all the birds had made up their minds,
Their sounds echoed high, all different kinds:
We shall follow you, our faithful guide,
To reach our beloved king, we shall fly by your side.

So the group took off on an unknown route,
led by the wise hoopoe, and the rest followed suit.

Swallowed by darkness,
Towards strange terrain
To meet a leader in the land
Where the great king reigns.

The Journey

During the journey
Thunder
Wind
Lightning.

Some birds tired halfway through
And opted to turn back rather than continue.

Many got lost in the valley's abyss,
Some devoured by monsters of the wilderness

(Dragons and demons lurking at every turn),
A scorching sun made their feathers burn.

Some sadly drowned in the ocean seas,
Others were hit by cold fronts that made them freeze.

Some perished on the mountain's peak,
Crushed by strong winds, they were too weak.

Some were distracted by wonders en route,
Stopped, got lost, unable to follow suit.

Some bickered, fought and were led astray,
Some were mesmerized by marvels on the way.
Of all the thousands of birds that had departed
Only thirty survived among those who had started.

The Arrival

After a thousand and one days of flight,
A glimpse of Qaf's peak appeared in sight,
A mountain unlike any the birds had ever seen,
Majestic, marvellous, emerald green,
On which tall leafy trees proudly swayed,
And on their branches exotic birds were displayed.

The group dispersed in every direction,
Seeking their king with grave attention.

They separated, searched, called out in a loud voice:
O King Simurgh, where are you? In you we rejoice.

And after seven days and seven nights
Of the longed-for Simurgh not a trace, not a sight.

The birds, dishevelled and distraught, despaired,
Began to sob inconsolably and declared:

Hoopoe, were your words a fairy tale?
A magical story or a dream?
A mystery, or desert mirage?

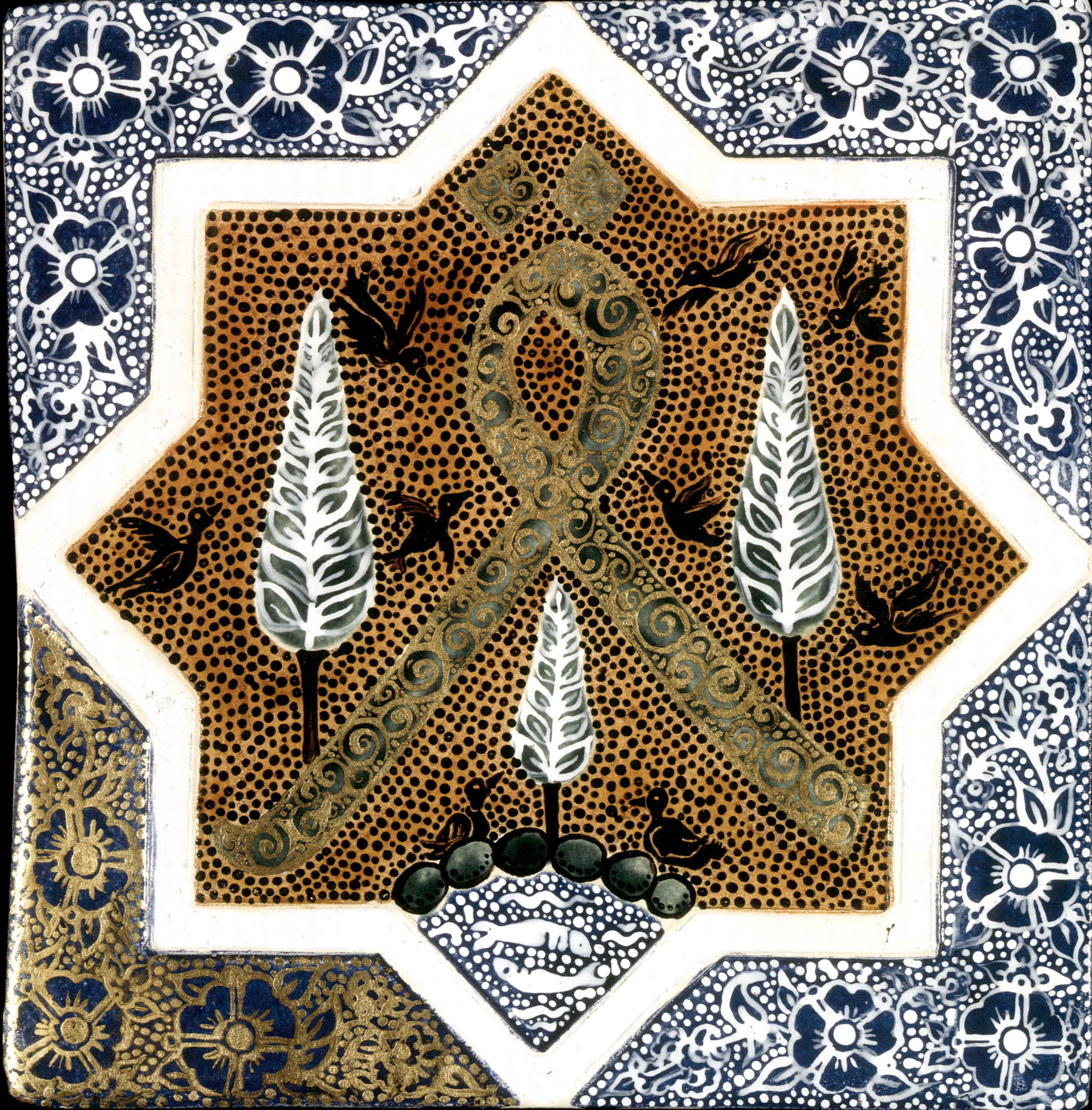

A cruel joke, or so it seems.

Weeping, crying, they all screeched in pain
Has this treacherous journey been in VAIN?!!!

When darkness fell and the moon shone bright
And stars shimmered brightly in Qaf's sky at night

The retinue gathered at a crystalline lake
To quench their thirst and lament their fate,
And as the birds bowed down to drink,
A vision on the water danced in the darkness and light.
The shadow of a huge majestic bird unveiled, a wondrous sight,
Engulfing within its wings the weary band of flight.

And as they stared in wonder at their mirrored reflection,
They saw themselves combined as one projection.

The thirty survivors appeared as one,
As shadows dissolving in the brilliant sun.

Their past, all what they had said or done,
Their doubts, their fears were now all gone.
Their souls and spirits were now purified,
Of worldly greed, vanity and foolish pride.

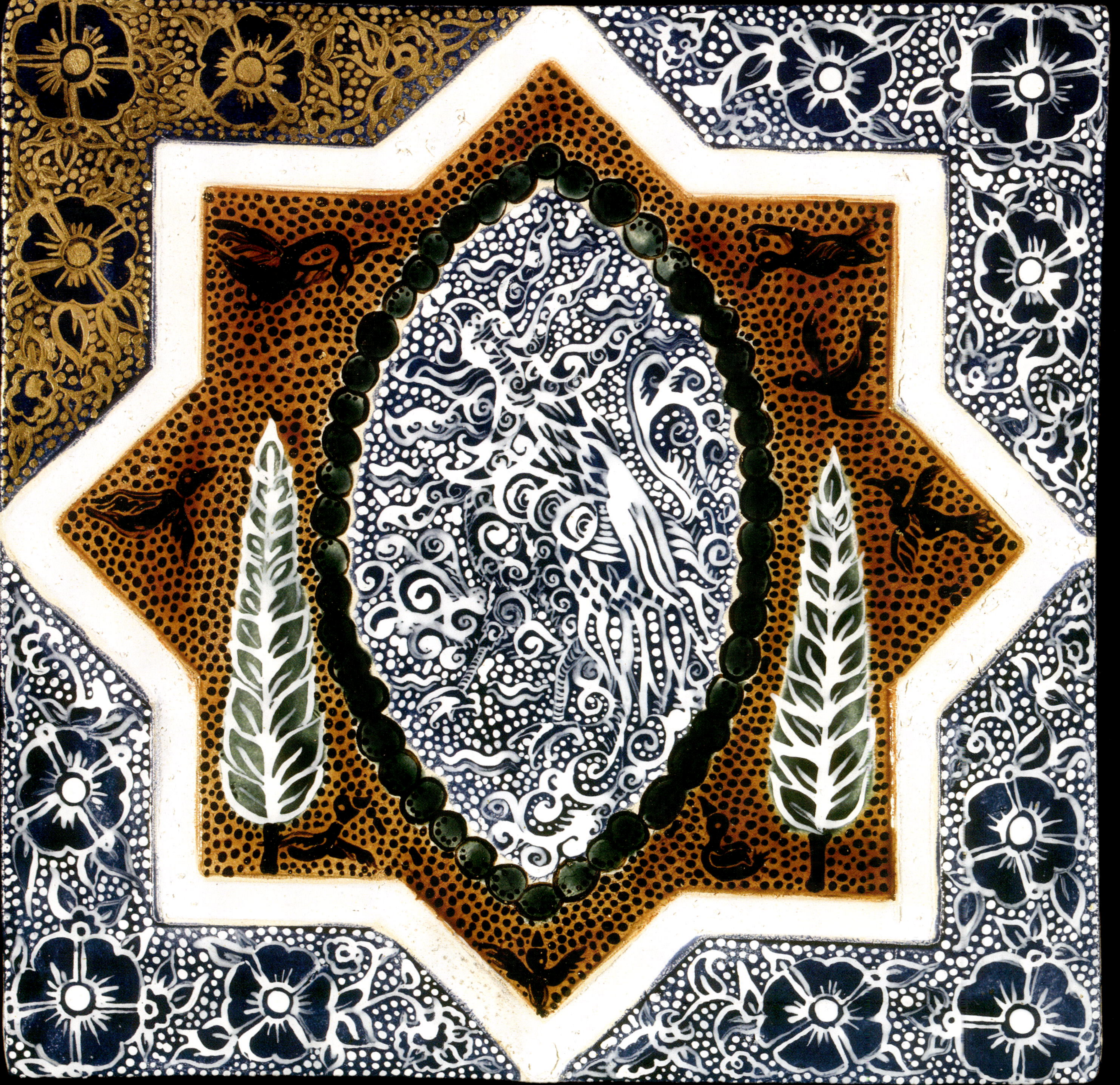

Slowly they began to understand that the suffering and pain
Endured on their long arduous journey was not in vain.

The veil had lifted, the truth transparent,
The secret of the quest became apparent.

They realized the treasure they came to find
Was not elsewhere but what they had left behind.

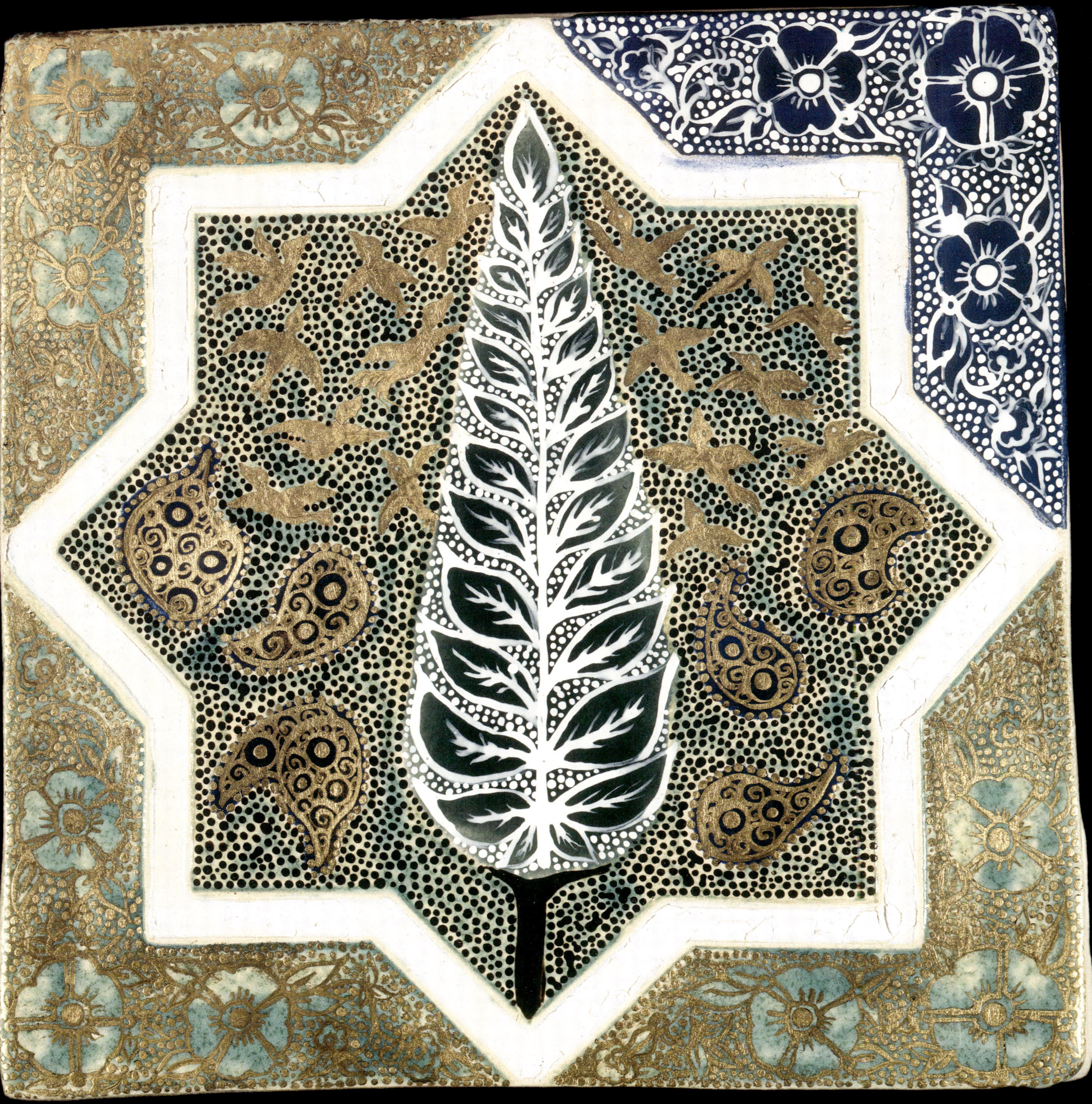

The Awakening

Peacock, without his mirror, lost his vanity and foolish pride,
Bulbul for his beloved rose no longer cried,
Duck, despite a throat parched and dry,
Gained sweet patience flying through the sky.

By giving up her precious jewels,
Partridge realized what a fool
She'd been to obsess with glitter and greed.
On a trip such trinkets she did not need.

Hawk regained his precious dignity,
Far from being a sultan's favourite frivolity.
Parrot discovered on each of the journey's stages
Liberty is sweeter than all delights of gilded cages.
The owl, who made new friends along the way,
Preferred their company to being alone all day.
At that moment the enlightened band of friends realized
That the desired goal does not live in foreign skies,
On mountain tops or in desert sands,
Across oceans, faraway seas or lands.
But the treasure they sought were virtues within themselves concealed,
And through this journey, each hidden jewel was finally revealed.

The Birds' Journey to Qaf

The tale takes place in ancient times, many many years ago, when all the birds of the world gather together to seek out an ideal king. The birds are living in tyranny and dream of a better world where they can live in peace, harmony and freedom. A wise bird, the hoopoe bird, tells them of the existence of a great wise ruler, a king of birds, the mighty Simurgh who lives across seven mountains and seven valleys on a mountain called Qaf. Intrigued by the story of Simurgh, the birds are at first eager to start the journey. However, upon realizing how long the trip will take, how uncertain the path and how distant the destination, the birds begin to offer excuses as to why not to go on the journey: the love-smitten nightingale cannot leave her beloved rose, the spoiled parrot cannot leave his life of comfort in his gilded cage, the duck cannot be separated from her water, the royal hawk will not part from the arm of his princely hunter, the reclusive owl cannot bear to go out in daylight with other birds. Persuaded by the hoopoe, the birds set out on their quest, but only those who are willing to sacrifice their past lives and rise above their doubts, fears, attachments, addictions and habits are able to cross the seven dangerous valleys to Mount Qaf.

And so the birds make their way, traversing across the valleys. Each valley presents a different challenge to the wayfarers. The first valley they come across is the Valley of the Quest where murderous dragons lurk, the second is the Valley of Love where all selfish love must be abandoned, the third is the Valley of Knowledge where roads take those on them around in circles and in different directions but never end anywhere. The fourth is the Valley of Detachment where they must detach from desire to possess all material things and where planets become as minute as sparks of dust and elephants are not distinguishable from ants. The fifth valley is the Valley of Oneness where all numbers add up to one. The sixth is the Valley of Bewilderment, a topsy-turvy world where all concepts are confused. The last valley is the Valley of Extinction, where each traveller has to submerge in one encompassing ocean.

After this treacherous journey, on which thousands had set out, only a select thirty birds make it across those valleys and reach the abode of Simurgh. As they descend Mount Qaf and after an extensive search, no trace of the elusive Simurgh is to be found. Exhausted, distraught and dumbfounded, the birds turn inwards in silence and examine their experience. As they look at a shadow in a lake, they realize that they themselves are Simurgh (meaning 'thirty birds' in Persian) and that Simurgh is the combination of them all, guiding them from within throughout the journey. In experiencing their joint quest, by conquering the challenges that faced them in each valley they crossed, they were able to dissolve boundaries and discover a common destiny. What they had set out to seek was within them all the time, but they were not able to realize that until they had been on the quest.

Faridudin Attar, a poet who lived in twelfth-century Neishapour, Persia, wrote his epic masterpiece *Mantiq at-Tayr* (*Conference of the Birds*) in about 4,000 lines of *Mathnawi* poetry (rhyming couplets). *Mantiq at-Tayr* is one of the most beautiful masterpieces of all Persian literature. Within the larger context of the story of the journey of the birds, Attar masterfully weaves anecdotes, parables, fables and subplots in a captivating poetic style. Powerful kings and princes, wise prophets and sages, love-smitten princesses and singing maidens, slaves, vagabonds and paupers are just some of the characters used to exemplify the two main Sufi themes that are prevalent throughout the poem: the necessity of renouncing the self and the search for divine unity. Attar, the grand master of storytelling, keeps his audience enthralled throughout, through his imagery, his wit and his colourful vignettes.

A Personal Quest

The process of writing *The Birds' Journey to Qaf* culminated in a marvellous quest of my own. The story, a hidden treasure, had to be revealed in an artistic way. The feathered characters beckoned to come alive in a visual representation that befitted the original context they appeared in. I knew I had found the right artist to convey the beauty of the narrative when I saw Vanessa Hodgkinson's exhibition in Kuwait in May 2004. Recently graduated from Cambridge, she was able to see beyond the perfection of geometric lines and the meticulous yet sometimes stifling impersonal form that is often associated with high Islamic art. Her art had a palpably Islamic and yet defiantly personal approach. Her juxtaposition of old and new, sacred and profane, east and west, English and Arabic strongly appealed to my own mixed Arab and English cultures. A dialogue ensued, a transcendence of boundaries, borders and barriers. An English version of the poem was almost simultaneously produced with the Arabic interpretation, which was the original language I perceived this project to be in. A few months later, after careful research of the project, Vanessa suggested a departure from the tradition of producing the illustrations on paper to a much more appropriately cultural and historical medium, that of Kashan ceramic tiles which were a typical feature of twelfth century iconography in the Islamic world. While both geometric and figurative representations adorned these tiles in architecture in the Islamic lands, some of them were also accompanied with poetic verses that suggest a highly aesthetic artistic function. Such poetic tiles became an inspiration for the project. And thus the menagerie of feathered friends had finally found the perfect medium of expression, a retelling of a twelfth-century medieval mystical fable on a replica of a twelfth-century decorative art form. An ancient tale has been reinterpreted, both textually and tactilely, with the strongest belief in the transcendent message the original poem conveys, that of a quest towards a common humanity.

Glossary

King Solomon: Prophet mentioned in the Qur'an empowered with command of winds and understanding the language of the birds.

Queen of Sheba 'Balqis': A powerful queen who ruled the land of Saba in Southern Arabia, present-day Yemen, mentioned in the Qur'an as a possessor of a mighty throne.

Hoopoe 'Hudhud': A Mediterranean bird known for its pale orange feathers tipped with black and a long thin crest on its head. Mentioned in the Qur'an as being a go-between, a messenger and bearer of letters between King Solomon and the Queen of Sheba asking the mighty queen to submit to one God.

Simurgh: A Persian word for a mythical bird described as the King of all Birds and possessor of magical properties also known as 'The Anqa' in Arabic and 'The Phoenix' in English.

Mount Qaf: Name of a world-encircling magical mountain that, according to some medieval Islamic geographers, is said to be made of emerald, surrounded by waters and extremely high.

Farid uddin al-Attar (1145–1221): One of the most famous Sufi poets in history. Lived in Nishapur, Persia, and is best known for his epic poem the *Mantiq at-Tayr*, a masterpiece of Persian literature.

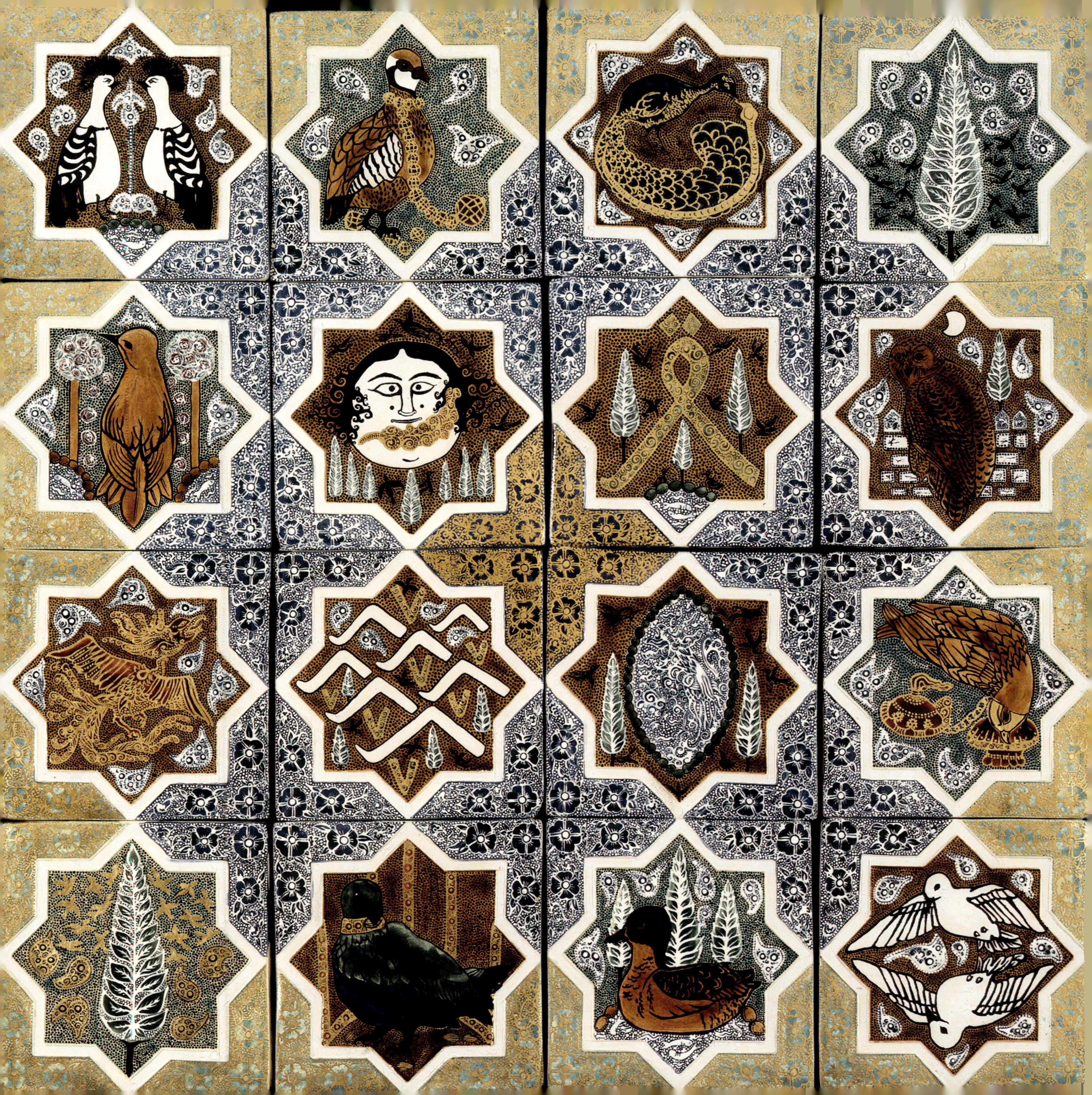